D1275524

'Judy ran out of life, but before that tragedy happened, it had run out on her.'

THE FILMS OF JUDY GARLAND

Brian Baxter

ISBN 0-912616-81-4

Greenhaven Press, Inc.
577 Shoreview Park Ave.
St. Paul, Minnesota 55112

Judy Garland had style. She also possessed magic. She became part of Hollywood as dream factory, and many would agree that she was – and remains – one of its mistreated masterpieces. Judy's talent, her limitations, her odd beauty are definable – her style and magic are not. Many artists reputedly have style; some apply it like make-up or a learned way of life, but in such cases it can prove all too transitory. Even the talented Miss Streisand will find that it cannot be dragged out of an expensive wardrobe, nor is it found in the footsteps of the great who have anticipated her.

Style has a lot to do with longevity and, despite her short life, Judy lived many times longer than we more ordinary mortals. Later, rather than sooner, style becames part of the star. This is why we admire and cherish the greats of Hollywood – Bogart, Gable, Tracy, Cooper, Garbo, Hepburn – and perhaps a few more. They possess a kind of radiance, that magical quality which the camera loves. It is something particularly noticeable when a star is most still, and if one recalls the most memorable screen moments of any actor, it is seldom the power-house scene, the big dramatic number. Rather it is – for Judy – the tranquil "Boy Next Door" song, the telephone scene in *I Could Go on Singing*, the lonely bar scene in *Easter Parade* or "It's a New World" from *A Star is Born*. These and other moments belong with Garbo at the end of *Queen Christina*, or Cooper buggying silently away at the end of *High Noon*. And with Bogart melancholy and drunk in *Casablanca*, or Tracy at his world-weary best in a dozen roles, proving himself the greatest actor ever to grace the screen.

Judy nurtured her style: indeed, as the years wore on, she relied on it as much as upon her increased technical skill, to hide the scars and loneliness and her diminishing abilities.

Of course, the magic never left her. As a child – the photographs and recent research testify – she could already captivate an audience just as she was to captivate Louis B Mayer. By her teens, she was a Hollywood star and the recipient of her only Academy Award. She had been placed on a treadmill, already considered both a seasoned performer and a piece of maleable property destined to work for MGM for fifteen long years. Judy's main film career did not just encompass those few years: it lasted through the two golden decades of Hollywood and spanned the two eras either side of World War II. Noel Simsolo in his monograph on Judy wrote: "The story of Judy Garland is the story of our society

Opposite: Frances Gumm, a star from childhood

and of our civilisation." It is a key remark to an understanding of Judy, her life and times. She was not *just* the possessor of unique qualities and talents, nor *just* the product of the movies and Hollywood. She reflected her time and place. Her rise and decline echo – or is it anticipate? – the decline of wit, grace and glamour from the movies, not least the musical. The ugly '60s could find no place for Judy and the disregard for *subtlety* in our present decade defies comment. In the early '50s it was possible for Judy to co-star opposite James Mason, whom Cukor allowed to act even with his back to the camera (see the parcel delivery scene after the "Somewhere There's a Someone" number). In the 1977 version, Kris Kristofferson has a cleavage that outplunges his co-star.

And so, while hoping to avoid pomposity, this little, detailed filmography charts a particular, marvellous career in the movies (not forgetting the other media which Judy conquered, or the concerts), while following a decline in all the very attributes that made her a star. Quite simply, there is no longer a place for those qualities in the movies nor – possibly – in our society and civilisation. Judy ran out of life, but before that tragedy happened, it had run out on her. Anyone who knows her only from a couple of over-played record tracks, the silly press and magazine articles or the disastrous British television shows of her last years, will never understand why she was the most loved of performers. Nor why she alone earned the title "Miss Show Business". And why – despite a million highs and lows – she could captivate any audience in the world.

Childhood gave way too soon to maturity and that maturity rapidly to something beyond the telling: a kind of lived-in experience (shared, for example, by Piaf and Monroe) which seems to beckon the personality to an early grave. Looking back over Judy's last years – the only time when I knew her at all personally – it is easy to see that life not only failed to *begin* at forty, it ebbed away. Her acting talent had never been greater (1962 is the year of *A Child is Waiting and I Could Go on Singing*), but already the style had been supplanted by mannerism. The wonderful talent exhausted her, the magic worked – but through allusion as well as illusion, through history as well as skill.

Her last professional engagements were not movies, and even guest appearances seemed unlikely to happen. She was to work briefly in Copenhagen and finally at The Talk of the Town in London, a month-long stint which she did not really

Opposte: recording with Frank Sinatra

CBS

enjoy, and where the tabloid press had a field day. Financially she was not well off; physically she was frail. Shortly after her forty-seventh birthday – on the Saturday night/Sunday morning, 21/22 June, she died. The offical cause, an accidental overdose of sleeping tablets. In truth she was worn out. In one way full of life and intelligence; in another tired beyond the heart's endurance.

During that week she had wanted to borrow one of her old MGM movies, most specifically *Meet Me in St Louis.* I had tried to get a 16mm copy for her, but Metro – generous to the last – had "no copy available". The best I could come up with was a vintage Hollywood comedy, *Bringing Up Baby*, which she never, in fact, projected. It was not a happy end to the fairy story of a child who became a legend in her early lifetime. But it seems strangely apt that both Metro and the gutter press should somehow be hovering in the wings, at the end, just as they had done most of her life.

Right: signing autographs outside the London Palladium. Opposite: waiting in the wings in I Could Go On Singing

Judy: the movies

Judy Garland was born on June 10, 1922 in Grand Rapids, Minnesota. She was the third daughter of Frank and Ethel Gumm, a fairly well-known music hall duo, who quickly incorporated Judy (christened Frances) and her sisters, Virginia and Mary, into the act. Judy's first appearance on the boards was when aged about two. It was not until nine years later, when a theatre proclaimed "The Glum Sisters" that Judy was re-christened. The show's producer, George Jessel, called her Garland after a New York critic friend of his, while Frances became Judy of her own choice – allegedly because of a currently popular Hoagy Carmichael tune.

When Judy was twelve, her father became ill and the family stopped touring. Her mother – a dominant force through Judy's early career and later life, and allegedly a very destructive one – took her to MGM Studios. For the only time in the studio's history, an artist was signed up without a screen test. Louis B Mayer heard the audition and the contract was issued, albeit at a nominal salary. Even so it was two years before Judy's screen debut, in a short with Deanna Durbin, the historic *Every Sunday*. In the meantime Frank Gumm had died – to Judy's great and lasting sorrow – and the sisters largely disappeared from her life. She was left, aged fourteen, to the far from tender mercies of a major studio, Hollywood at large and an ambitious mother.

The little two-reeler caused no particular excitement and MGM let Deanna Durbin move to Universal with Judy staying (thanks to the support of Arthur Freed and Roger Edens) with the big company. Strangely, her feature debut was not with MGM but in a mild musical comedy (football-oriented) on loan to 20th Century-Fox. The movie, *Pigskin Parade*, was her only work outside Metro until her dismissal some fifteen years later. In *Pigskin Parade* she sang three songs, received a charitable note in the New York Times ("a pleasingly fetching personality") and the next year made her breakthrough in Roy del Ruth's *Broadway Melody of 1938*, which had a fairly strong cast, with Judy taking seventh billing. The knock-out number was, of course, "You Made Me Love You". Judy sings this song with a special introduction and interpolation – to Clark Gable. The unaffected simplicity of the sequence is part of the magic:

Opposite: as Dorothy in The Wizard of Oz

the treatment is one that has given Judy some of her greatest moments. Gentle, uncluttered and relying on that instinctive talent and ability to produce sentiment without sentimentality. The film was not great, but Bosley Crowther in the New York Times could write: "The idea and words are almost painfully silly – yet Judy puts it over – in fact with a bang." The next years mark Judy's busiest period. The relentless years from 1937 until 1942 when, in *For Me and My Gal*, she was the only name listed above the film's title. She had arrived. But the journey had covered five strenuous years, a dozen films, and it had sown the seeds of her fame and destruction.

The first of these twelve movies is an enjoyable little comedy drama, *Thoroughbreds Don't Cry*, about two boys trying to train a horse. It's important as the first of her eight films with her life-long friend, the indefatigable Mickey Rooney. Basically a film for the young audience, it is really Rooney's film, since he was already a more established and experienced screen performer. This was the period of the child actor – Deanna Durbin, Freddie Bartholemew, Shirley Temple and Jackie Cooper. Rather significantly, the same year introduced the rather older and certainly tougher Dead End Kids.

Next came the aptly titled *Everybody Sing*, where Judy took third place to Allan Jones and Fanny Brice. She was very lively, in the swing style of that period and her popularity was increasing daily – with critics and public alike.

There followed another movie for the same director, playing with Freddie Bartholemew. *Listen Darling* is the better movie and the adult leads were Mary Astor (later her mother in *Meet Me in St Louis*) and Walter Pidgeon. Songs here included "Zing Went the Strings of My Heart" and "On the Bumpy Road to Love", both signifying the juvenile romance elements that were to creep into Judy's parts. She was being effectively groomed and, within the same year (1938), Metro wrote her into one of the very popular Andy Hardy Series: in *Love Finds Andy Hardy*. The musical numbers are rather tacked on, but the most famous is probably the little lament, "In Between", which summed up Judy's predicament. She was well into her teens, had a fantastic talent as a singer, an emergent one as an actress and unspoiled looks.

Opposite: with Ethel Gumm, her mother, a dominant and ambitious force in Judy's career

But they were increasingly mature looks which nearly lost her what became the most important single film of her career, the immortal *The Wizard of Oz*, made by Victor Fleming just before he went on to complete *Gone With the Wind*. Judy

was tightly corseted, and pigtailed, to play the part of young Dorothy, for she herself was just seventeen. It's well known that Metro wanted Shirley Temple for the main part, and also that the "Over the Rainbow" sequence was very nearly cut of the final print. Luckily neither happened.

This musical fantasy is a timeless masterpiece. How it happened will always remain a mystery – it is simply one of the miraculous examples of the many wonderful parts adding up to a magnificent whole. It won Judy her only Academy Award, a special as "best juvenile performer of the year". The movie could not be bettered and it's strange that Fleming – not an especially gifted director – should have had a large hand in creating two films that can never be re-made, (not that some misguided person won't try, of course). *The Wizard of Oz* stems from a classic story and is made with a skill, devotion and lavishness which do not quite account for its success. No science fiction has ever equalled it and bizarrely – for all the potential of cinema – no fantasy has approached it. The film delights new cinema audiences each year, and proves a timeless standby on both British and American television.

The lasting significance of the movie is that Judy was a star and she rapidly went into *Babes in Arms*, with Mickey Rooney, under the guidance of that overrated talent, Busby Berkeley. In 1940 another Andy Hardy venture (Rooney's ninth) saw her teamed as the juvenile lead for almost the last time. She was now eighteen, prettier than ever, and becoming increasingly sophisticated. Songs in *Andy Hardy Meets Debutante* included "I'm Nobody's Baby" and "Alone". This same year Judy was overworked into a bright musical *Strike Up the Band*, under the producership of Arthur Freed and once again musically supervised by Roger Edens. At the end of that year there came an odd departure. Judy played a double role (mother and daughter) in the screen version of George M Cohan's *Little Nellie Kelly*. It allowed her to grow up and to play the only death-bed scene of her career. According to her co-star, George Murphy, the scene totally knocked out the studio personnel and although the movie seems rather sentimental and drawn out now, it's important as a dramatic first, and for several songs with which we associate Judy, especially "A Pretty Girl Milking Her Cow".

Murphy's account of the shooting comes as no surprise, since Judy has always been greatly admired by her professionals and many have paid generous tribute to her over the years (a

Opposite: with Gene Kelly in For Me and My Gal. Overleaf: with Margaret O'Brien in Meet Me in St Louis

few have, with reason, complained at the waiting and troubles on set), not least Gene Kelly, James Mason and Howard Keel. The last named was particularly kind about Judy on a BBC radio porgramme and seemed to hold no ill-feeling about the problems that occurred on the aborted version of *Annie Get Your Gun*.

While talking about professionals, readers may be interested in a small personal story that illustrates the effect Judy could have upon an attentive audience. It occurred on a Sunday morning, the day of Dirk Bogarde's John Player lecture at the National Film Theatre in London. We decided to have a run-through of the film clips to be shown during the afternoon discussion. One selected was the climactic scene between Judy and Dirk at the end of *I Could Go on Singing*. Selected not for his performance, but to illustrate his work on the film and the help he had given to his co-star. A host of BBC technicians and other professionals were in the NFT arranging lights for the programme to be filmed. At the end of that seven-minute clip the entire audience burst spontaneously into applause. No-one could say that it was for Bogarde, since his involvement in the scene is very much on the side-lines. It was, indisputably, for Judy's magnificent performance. It is a sad thought that our filmography stops in the early '60s.

After *Little Nellie Kelly*, there followed the much more lavish and colourful *The Ziegfeld Girl*, with Judy in competition with Lana Turner and Hedy Lamarr. It was during this year that Judy, then nineteen, married musician David Rose. A clip from *Ziegfeld Girl* was released as *We Must Have Music*, explaining, with Garland numbers, the work of a studio's music department. The breakneck pace continued with the last of her three Andy Hardy sagas and the rather overlong *Babes on Broadway* with Judy and Mickey successfully invading the big time. She worked again for Busby Berkeley in a war-time piece to help boost morale, *For Me and My Gal*. It's important as the film that expressly said: "Judy Garland in . . . " The two male leads were Gene Kelly, making his screen debut, and George Murphy. Although one of many backstage musical variations, it moves away from the conventions and becomes wildly over-dramatic, allowing Kelly to be heroic and, of course, to end up with Judy. Her solo songs included the memorable "After You've Gone" and "How You Gonna Keep 'Em Down on the Farm".

There were a couple more films during the first part of her

Opposite: with Mickey Rooney in Girl Crazy

three-phase career, both in 1943, plus a guest appearance in the multi-star *Thousands Cheer*, where she sang "The Joint is Jumpin' – Down at Carnegie Hall". Enough said, except to note that, a decade or two later, she kept her promise to us and Carnegie Hall, with the greatest single concert success of her career.

The two intervening movies were both rather good. *Presenting Lily Mars* began as a straight film for Lana Turner (it derives from a Booth Tarkington novel) and became a lively musical drama, produced by her loyal supporter Joe Pasternak and efficiently directed by Norman Taurog. It was retrograde in keeping back her obvious maturity, but otherwise had charm and a nutty inconsequence that typified much of her work during that period. The same may be said of the more zestful *Girl Crazy* which was her last film with Mickey Rooney as full co-star. Direction was again by Taurog, but the grand finale was by Berkeley and Judy's dance numbers were staged by Charles Walters who was later to direct her. She had truly arrived: three people to look after directorial aspects, Edens and George Stoll to look after the music, with the original songs (including "Embracable You" and "But Not For Me") by George and Ira Gershwin. It was the precursor to her less prolific, but richest MGM period. The time of her divorce, after barely two years, from David Rose and the Vincente Minnelli years. A period which witnessed her marriage to the great director, the birth of her first child, Liza, and the ten films which mark her maturity as a performer. The period also marks her physical collapse and the paying of the price that these earlier years had extracted.

Despite the first marriage, the second to Minnelli and the subsequent arrival of Liza, the studio did not really want Judy to grow up. She played a seventeen year-old in the enchanting *Meet Me in St Louis*, shy and in love with the boy next door. She was then twenty-one and had been on the boards or in front of cameras for eighteen years. Still, in film terms, the best was yet to come – particularly this sentimental, but never sickly, family musical set in turn-of-the-century St Louis. It contains the famous "Trolley Song", "Have Yourself a Merry Little Christmas" and the title song. There's also the remarkable "The Boy Next Door", which Minnelli shoots almost straight, giving Judy the song, the entire sequence uninterrupted. Importantly he directed Judy in her next movie – and her first straight role. *Under the Clock* is a very simple war-time romantic drama. A

Opposite: top hat and tails for Judy and Mickey Rooney, close friends and co-stars through six films

country-boy soldier (Robert Walker) meets a girl during a two-day break in New York (used as the film's third star). They fall in love, get parted, reunited and married. To be honest, the script and the war-time mood have dated it now. But not the freshness of Walker's portrayal or the delicate sincerity of Judy as Alice. Minnelli's fluid camera and exciting use of the backgrounds, are great props to the inexperienced straight actress and he helped her avoid falling back on mannerism or tricks. One is only happy that Fred Zinnemann did not complete the film, having begun it and "not got on" with Judy.

Whatever the success of *Under the Clock*, the public – and Metro – wanted Judy to sing. Also in this immediate post-war period, colour, fantasy and excitement were needed, not small-scale black and white dramas, starring MGM's greatest singing star. She quickly went into a lively musical-western, based on the story of the pioneer waitresses, *The Harvey Girls*. It stands up well today, mostly because director George Sidney doesn't take it over-seriously, and allows Judy some of her funniest moments to date. The film was an enormous financial success and Judy Garland was reputedly earning several thousand dollars a week at this time. MGM whizzed

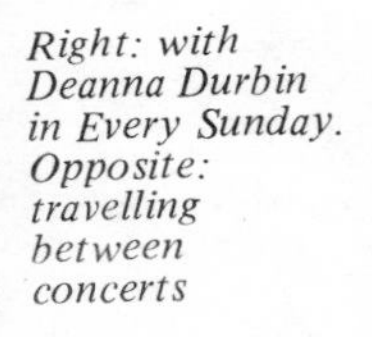

Right: with Deanna Durbin in Every Sunday. Opposite: travelling between concerts

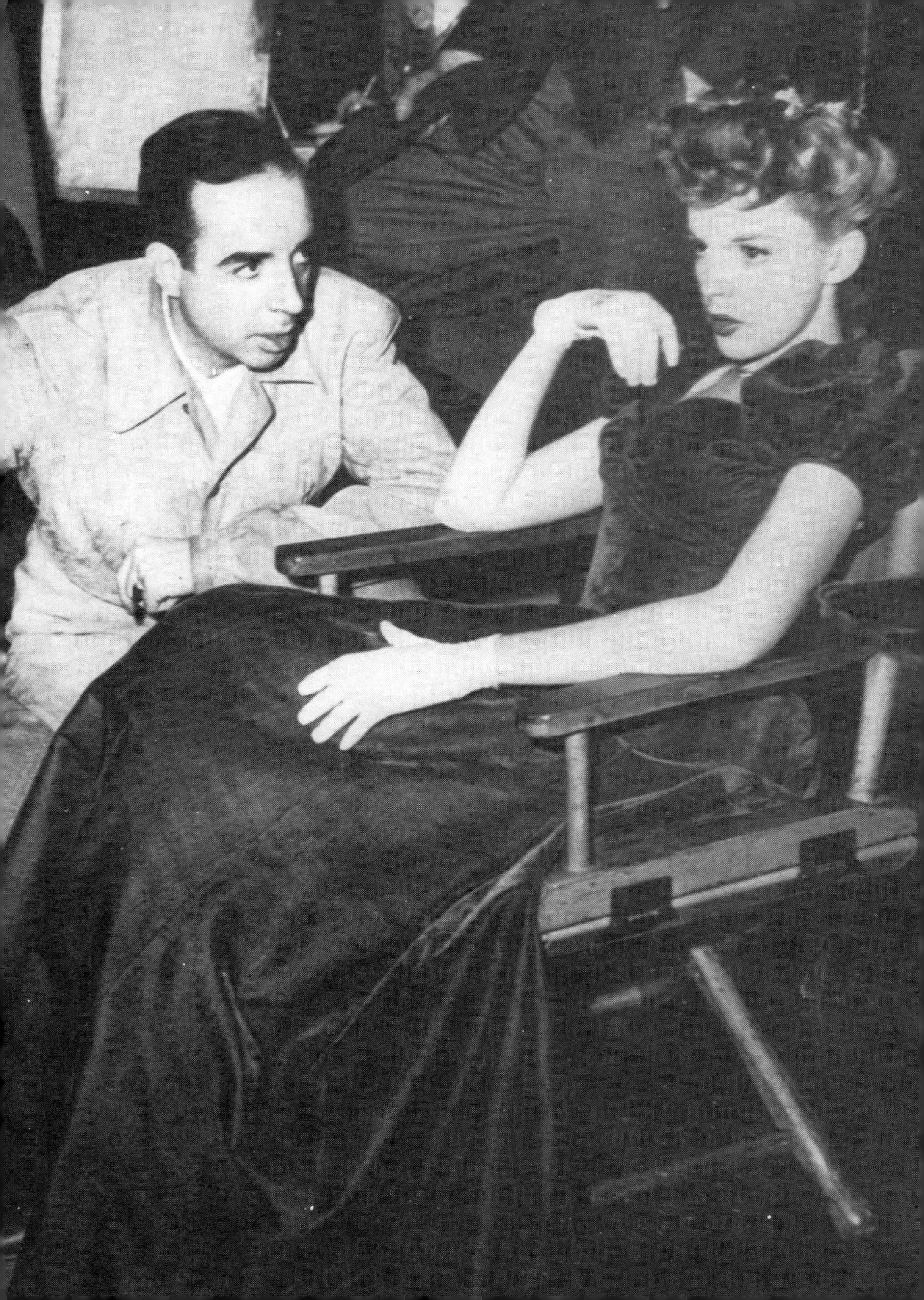

Right: with final husband Mickey Deans. Opposite: on set with director Vincente Minnelli, who became her second husband

her into the life story of Jerome Kern, *Till The Clouds Roll By*, but she was already pregnant. Thankfully Minnelli directed the sequences and although none of them is as good as her marvellous number, "The Great Lady Gives an Interview" in *Ziegfeld Follies of 1946*, they are by far the best fifteen minutes in an otherwise dull movie. Interestingly, the sophisticated "interview" number and *The Pirate*, made after Liza's birth, were not liked by the fans, or even some critics. Straight comedy was acceptable, but evidently not the stylish satire which Judy had now mastered. She and Gene Kelly co-starred in the latter film which was then underrated and is now in danger of being overrated. The Cole Porter score includes "Love of My Life" and the lively duo, "Be A Clown", a precursor of the great "A Couple of Swells", which remains one of the highlights of her next musical, *Easter Parade*, directed by the sympathetic Charles Walters, who replaced Minnelli.

She took top billing over Fred Astaire in the movie, which had previously been a vehicle for Gene Kelly, until he broke his ankle. Judy traditionally received first billing over her male co-stars – not the usual Hollywood pattern. The film is a success, full of inspired moments, and whole sequences revealing that even though not *looking* her best, Judy had reached a new maturity. Howard Barnes in the New York Herald Tribune even wrote of it as her best performance to date. Certainly it was another box-office smash hit – and a few months previously, at the end of *The Pirate*, Judy had been committed to a private sanitorium. Her depressions and constant insomnia seem gradually to have worsened as the '40s wore on.

After *Easter Parade* another Garland-Astaire film was scheduled, but she never got to complete *The Berkeleys of Broadway*, so the next picture was guesting with Mickey Rooney in *Words and Music*, playing herself. The problems with the studio were at their worst pitch during 1948, but in 1949 Metro cast her in the musical re-make of Lubitsch's *The Shop Around the Corner*, now retitled *In the Good Old Summertime*. Despite weight and temperament fluctuating wildly, the film is a personal success for its star, and the script gives her good opportunities to act, the songs often taking second place. It's another attractive nostalgia piece, not totally dissimilar to *St Louis* in feeling. It proved to be her last MGM picture, except for *Summer Stock* (GB title: *If You Feel Like Singing*) with her friend, Gene Kelly. Actually it is not at all bad – largely thanks to Charles Walters' musical numbers, and the fantastic "Get Happy" finale, which was (incorrectly) rumoured to be from earlier period. The weight problem was very marked on this picture, and her loyal friend and frequent producer, Joe Pasternak, obviously had a great deal of trouble in completing the movie.

It was to be the end of an era. Other projects around this period, *Royal Wedding*, which was to follow *Summer Stock, Showboat* and, of course, *Annie Get Your Gun*, all ended up with different female leads: Jane Powell, Ava Gardner and Betty Hutton respectively. The last named had a score actually recorded by Judy, but the issued record does not inspire one to believe that the film would have been among her most memorable. In the event MGM wound up her contract and although one can understand some of the reasons, many people felt that a star who had worked on some thirty films, earning a reputed thirty-six million dollars for the studio, deserved better treatment.

The discussion over the studio treatment of Judy Garland will never end. Certainly few would deny that she cost MGM much time and trouble in the second phase of her film career, after *St Louis* and *The Clock*. So many people were loyal to her that to talk about the studio as a monster is obviously inappropriate. At least opportunities were made and people such as Walters, Pasternak and Kelly helped in those latter MGM days. Two facts remain. Certainly Judy was worked and pushed far too hard in the very late '30s and early '40s

Oppsoite: with her first child, Liza Minnelli. Overleaf: with first husband David Rose

and the detailed research that has gone into the period shows the heavy dependence on stimulants and depressants, which were to affect her health then and later. The other fact is that no financial allowance seems to have been made for fifteen years and some thirty movies. The movies – particularly *The Wizard of Oz* – like the records, went on making money. Many of her financial problems and the need to take on certain unsatisfactory engagements could perhaps have been avoided by legitimate royalties from discs and some form of pension from MGM after the late '40s.

This was not to be, and the following years saw a final dissolution of the Garland-Minnelli marriage, some while after a much-publicised suicide attempt. This brief film biography takes a halt now, since its concentration is mainly on Judy Garland's films. But before mentioning the last great film work of her career, it is, of course, essential to remember that records, live shows, radio and, later, television, kept her busy for months on end. A few of the radio shows have been issued as recordings. Some (but not all her twenty-six hour-long shows) television spectaculars have been seen in Britain. The records are, of course, legion. But it was the live concerts that kept her busiest – and financially solvent – over the next years. Importantly there was the first Palladium show in early 1951, staged by Charles Walters, and written for her by Roger Edens. This led to the great Palace comeback: the "five-week" stint that began in October 1951 and ran for nineteen weeks to capacity houses, taking – according to Variety – 750,000 dollars at the box office. The show continued and Judy married Sid Luft in 1952, her third husband. She had two children of that marriage, Lorna (1952) then Joe (1955).

Naturally one regrets that some of the records of live shows do less than justice to the concerts and Judy was even displeased by the occasional shrillness of her magnificent Carnegie Hall double album. Equally tragic is the fact that there is so little television material in colour. The sad "Sunday Night at the Palladium" does not bear remembering and anyone who attended the Judy and Liza concert at the Palladium will know that the television programme made from the show was little short of disastrous. The performances were simply too big and too personal to be put over on the small screen.

Opposite: preparing for the "Be a Clown" number in The Pirate

I was fortunate to see Judy, live, on several occasions, most notably at the Palladium and on one incredible occasion at

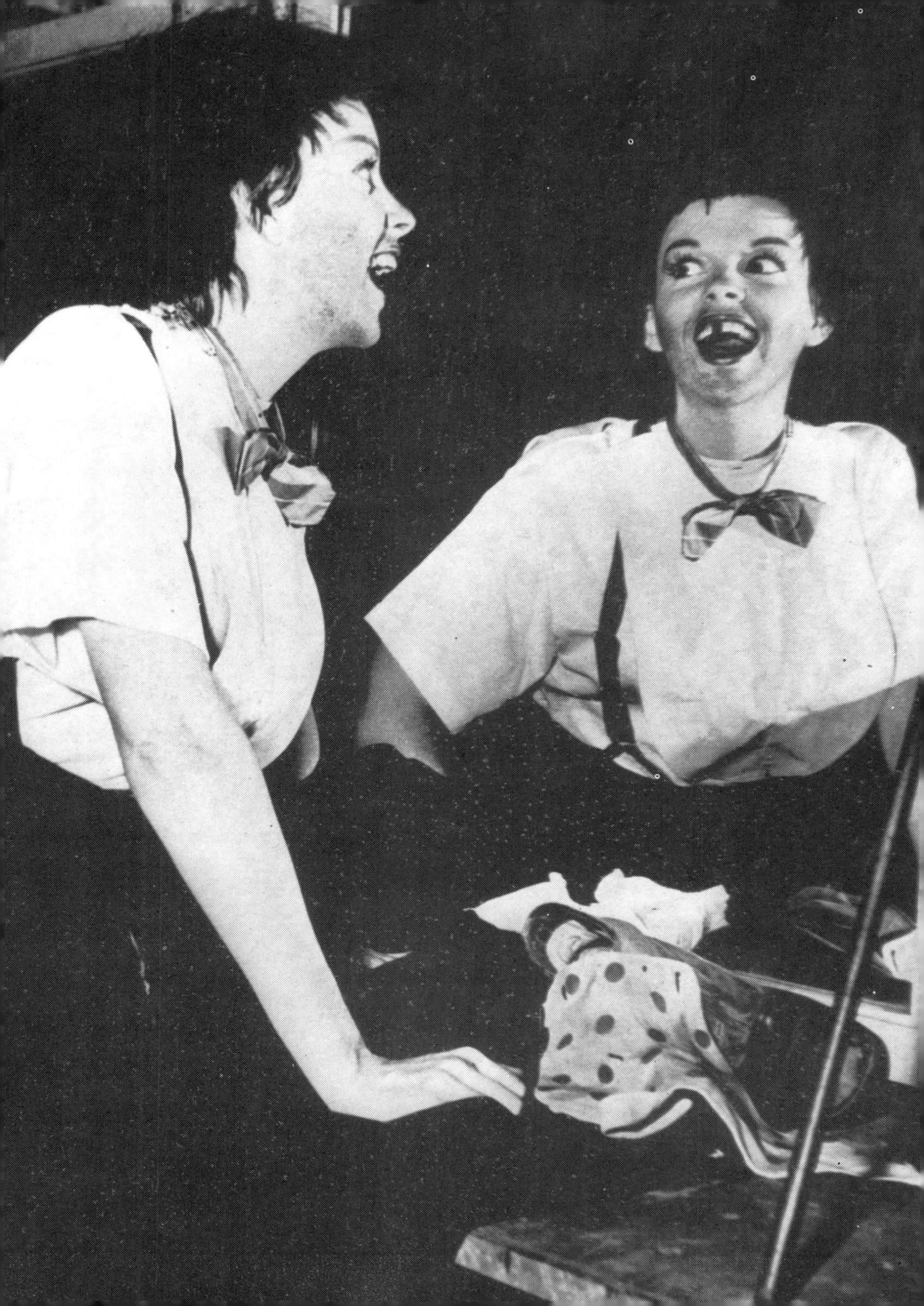

the Hollywood Bowl, where 18,000 people braved massive parking problems, delays and – uncharacteristically – a very damp evening to enjoy the concert of a lifetime. One cannot adequately convey the excitement and tension of such an event, and certainly no recording can capture the (seeming) spontanaeity of the repartee, the little dances, the encores.

However, this particular concert, one of so many, comes after the birth of the children and certainly after her return to the screen in the musical re-make of *A Star is Born*. The film was produced by Luft and directed by George Cukor, who – along with Minnelli – is the only great director she was to work with. The movie cost five million dollars, took months to shoot and – unbelievably – failed to win Judy the Academy Award for best actress. Even in the finally released version, it's a long work. A magnificient back-stage story about the decline of an alcoholic actor and the parallel rise to fame of his wife. James Mason is superb as Norman Maine, the star who eventually commits suicide, and Judy gives what Time described as, "just about the greatest one-woman show in modern movie history." Even so, it was years before the next movie came along.

There were innumerable records, television shows and

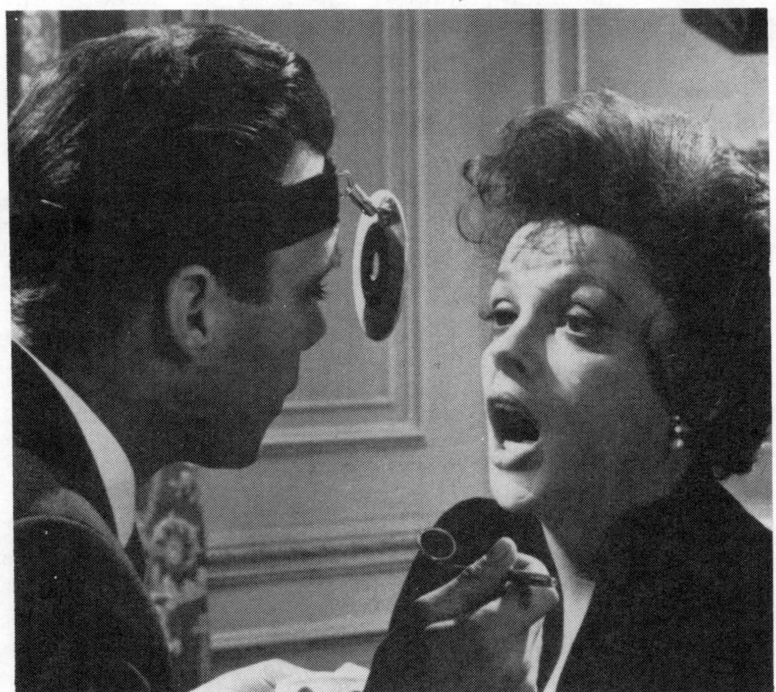

Right: with Dirk Bogarde in I Could Go On Singing. Opposite: in Judgment at Nuremburg

concerts and cabaret appearances, then a soundtrack for *Pepe*. Until 1961 that was it – and the guest star appearance in Stanley Kramer's *Judgment at Nuremberg*, for which she received an Academy Award nomination as best supporting actress. It's a deeply affecting, straight appearance as a war victim. The next year she did the main voice (Mewsette) for a feature cartoon, *Gay Purr-ee* and then again for Kramer (producing only) she took the lead in John Cassavetes' *A Child is Waiting*. The film was not a popular success – concerned as it was with working with mentally retarded children – but her performance is intelligent and restrained. Strangely, it's another very straight role (playing a music teacher), though the period of the very late '50s and early '60s mark her greatest concert success – at the Palladium, Carnegie Hall and the Hollywood Bowl. They also mark her last film – her only one made in Britain – *I Could Go on Singing*.

The story is ordinary – a famous singer comes to London to see her estranged husband (Dirk Bogarde) and the son who thinks his mother is dead. Neither the triteness nor flat direction matters, since the whole thing revolves around Judy and the sympathetic support given by Bogarde, as the husband. The film is one of the truest to aspects of her own personality – plus hints of her actual life – and it captures the back-stage elements well. There is a final sequence when she has the camera to herself, explaining that she simply can't give another performance. The scene lasts most of a single reel, several minutes in fact. Various reports about the shooting have circulated – from director Ronald Neame, from her generous co-star Dirk Bogarde and from others who worked peripherally on the film. How it was shot matters little, since it retains two important qualities which transcend the actual shooting. Apart from a day on *Valley of the Dolls*, it marks her last film work. It also contains probably her greatest screen acting. Whatever the problems on the movie, whatever the box-office receipts, there remains the apt remark of a distinguished lady critic, who – reviewing the film in Sight and Sound – was able to conclude: "There's no counterfeiting that kind of talent." And on that succinct remark, rests Judy Garland's career, both in and out of the movies. Difficult, wayward, funny, tragic, talented. It doesn't matter *how* we remember Judy, the fact remains that she is irreplacable and she remains uncopiable – there *really* is no counterfeiting that very special talent.

Opposite: on stage in I Could Go On Singing

Filmography

EVERY SUNDAY
US 1936

Production/MGM. Two-reel short. B&W.

With: Deanna Durbin, Judy Garland

PIGSKIN PARADE
(GB: HARMONY PARADE)
US 1936

Producer/Darryl F Zanuck. Director/David Butler. Script/Harry Tugend, Jack Yellan, William Conselman. Music and lyrics/Lew Pollack, Sidney Mitchell and The Yacht Club Boys. Photography/Arthur Miller. B&W. GB distribution/20th Century-Fox. Certificate U. 90 mins.

With: Patsy Kelly (Bessie Winters), Jack Haley (Sling Winters), The Yacht Club Boys (Themselves), Stuart Erwin (Amos Dodd), John Downs (Chip Carson), Betty Grable (Laura Watson), Arline Judge (Sally Saxon), Dixie Dunbar (Ginger Jones), Judy Garland (Sairy Dodd)

BROADWAY MELODY OF 1938
US 1937

Producer/Jack Cummings. Director/Roy Del Ruth. Script/Jack McGowan. Music and lyrics/Nacio Herb Brown, Arthur Freed. Musical director/George Stoll. Musical arranger/Roger Edens. Photography/William Daniels. B&W. GB distribution/CIC (MGM). Certificate U. 109 mins.

With: Robert Taylor (Steve Raleigh), Eleanor Powell (Sally Lee), George Murphy (Sonny Ledford), Binnie Barnes (Caroline Whipple), Buddy Ebsen (Peter Trot), Sophie Tucker (Alice Clayton), Judy Garland (Betty Clayton), Charles Igor Gorin (Nicki Papaloopas), Raymond Walburn (Herman Whipple)

THOROUGHBREDS DON'T CRY
US 1937

Producer/Harry Rapf. Director/Alfred E Green. Script/Lawrence Hazard. Music and lyrics/Nacio Herb Brown, Arthur Freed. Photography/Leonard Smith. B&W. GB distribution/CIC (MGM). Certificate U. 80 mins.

With: Judy Garland (Cricket West), Mickey Rooney (Timmie Donovan), Sophie Tucker (Mother Ralph), C Aubrey Smith (Sir Peter Calverton), Robert Sinclair (Roger Calverton), Forrester Harvey (Wilkins)

EVERYBODY SING
US 1938

Producer/Harry Rapf. Director/Edwin L Marin. Script/Florence Ryerson, Edgar Allan Woolf. Music and lyrics/Bronislau Kaper, Walter Jurmann, Gus Kahn, Bert Kalmar, Harry Ruby. Photography/Joseph Ruttenberg. B&W. GB distribution/CIC (MGM). Certificate U. 91 mins.

With: Allan Jones (Ricky Saboni), Judy Garland (Judy Bellaire), Fanny Brice (Olga Chekaloff), Reginald Owen (Hillary Bellaire), Billie Burke (Diana Bellaire), Reginald Gardiner (Jerrold Hope), Lynn Carter (Sylvia Bellaire), Helen Troy (Secretary)

LISTEN DARLING
US 1938

Producer/Jack Cummings. Director/Edward L Marin. Script/Elaine Ryan, Anne Morrison Chapin. Music and lyrics/Al Hoffman, Al Lewis, Murray Mencher, Joseph McCarthy, Milton Ager, James F Henley. Photography/Charles Lawton Jnr. B&W. GB distribution/CIC (MGM). Certificate U. 75 mins.

With: Freddie Bartholomew (Buzz Mitchell), Judy Garland (Pinkie Wingate), Mary Astor (Dotty Wingate), Walter Pidgeon (Richard Thurlow), Alan Hale (J J Slattery)

LOVE FINDS ANDY HARDY
US 1938

Production/MGM. Director/George B Seitz. Script/William Indwig. Music and lyrics/Mack Gordon, Harry Revel, Roger Edens. Photography/Lester White. B&W. GB distribution/CIC (MGM). Certificate U. 91 mins.

With: Lewis Stone (Judge James Hardy), Mickey Rooney (Andrew Hardy), Judy Garland (Betsy), Cecilia Parker (Marian Hardy), Fay Holden (Mrs Hardy), Ann Rutherford (Polly Benedict), Betty Ross Clarke (Aunt Milly), Lana Turner (Cynthia)

THE WIZARD OF OZ
US 1939

Producer/Mervyn LeRoy. Director/Victor Fleming. Script/Noel Langley,

Opposite: in The Wizard of Oz

S INC.

Florence Ryerson. Edgar Allan Woolf. Music/Harold Arlen. Lyrics/E Y Harburg. Photography/Harold Rossen. Colour. GB distribution/CIC (MGM). Certificate U. 98 mins.

With: Judy Garland (Dorothy Gale), Frank Morgan (The Wizard), Ray Bolger (Scarecrow), Bert Lahr (Cowardly Lion), Jack Haley (Tin (Tin Man), Billie Burke (Glinda), Margaret Hamilton (Miss Gulch), Charles Grapewin (Uncle Henry)

BABES IN ARMS
US 1939

Producer/Arthur Freed. Director/ Busby Berkeley. Script/Jack McGowan, Kay Van Riper. Music/Rodgers & Hart, Nacio Herb Brown, Arthur Freed, Harold Arlen, E Y Harburg. Photography/Ray June. B&W. GB distribution/CIC (MGM). Certificate U. 96 mins.

With: Mickey Rooney (Mickey Moran), Judy Garland (Patsy Barton), Charles Winninger (Charles Moran), Guy Kibbie (Judge Black), June Preisser (Rosalie Essex), Grace Hoyes (Florrie Moran), Betty Janes (Molly Moran), Douglas MacPhail (Don Brice), Rand Brooks (Jeff Steele), Leni Lynn (Dody Martini)

ANDY HARDY MEETS DEBUTANTE
US 1940

Production/MGM. Director/George B Seitz. Script/Annalee Whitmore, Thomas Seller. Photography/Sidney Wagner, Charles Lawton. B&W. GB distribution/CIC (MGM). Certificate U. 87 mins.

With: Lewis Stone (Judge Hardy), Mickey Rooney (Andy Hardy), Cecilia Parker (Marian Hardy), Fay Holden (Mrs Hardy), Judy Garland (Betsy Booth), Ann Rutherford (Polly Benedict), Diana Lewis (Daphne Fowler), George Breakstone (Breezy)

STRIKE UP THE BAND
US 1940

Producer/Arthur Freed. Director/ Busby Berkeley. Script/John Monks Jnr, Fred Finklehoffe. Music and lyrics/ Roger Edens, George and Ira Gershwin. Photography/Ray June. B&W. GB distribution/CIC (MGM), Certificate U. 119 mins.

With: Mickey Rooney (Jimmy Connors), Judy Garland (Mary Holden), Paul Whiteman (Himself), June Preisser (Barbara Frances Morgan), William Tracey (Philip Turner), Larry Nunn (Willie Brewster), Margaret Early (Annie), Ann Shoemaker (Mrs Connors), Francis Pierlot (Mr Judd), Virginia Brissac (Mrs Mary Holden)

LITTLE NELLIE KELLY
US 1940

Prdoucer/Arthur Freed. Director/ Norman Taurog. Script/Jack McGowan, based on the musical by George M Cohan. Photography/Ray June. B&W. GB distribution/CIC (MGM). Certificate U. 98 mins.

With: Judy Garland (Nellie Kelly/Little Nellie Kelly), Charles Winninger (Michael Noonan), Douglas MacPhail (Dennis Fogarty), Arthur Shields (Timothy), Rita Page (Mary)

ZIEGFELD GIRL
US 1941

Producer/Pandro S Berman. Director/ Robert Z Leonard. Script/Marguerite Roberts, Sonya Levien. Music and lyrics/ Nacio Herb Brown, Gus Kahn, Roger Edens, Harry Carroll, Joseph McCarthy, Edward Gallagher, Al Sheen. Photography/Ray June. B&W. GB distribution/CIC (MGM). Certificate A. 132 mins.

With: James Stewart (Gilbert Young), Judy Garland (Susan Gallagher), Hedy Lamarr (Sandra Kolter), Lana Turner (Sheila Regan), Tony Martin (Frank Merton), Jackie Cooper (Jerry Regan), Ian Hunter (Geoffrey Collis), Charles Winninger (Pop Gallagher)

LIFE BEGINS FOR ANDY HARDY
US 1941

Production/MGM. Director/Gegorge B Seitz, Script/Agnes Christine Johnston. Music/Gegorge Stoll. Photography/ Lester White. B&W. GB distribution/ CIC (MGM). Certificate U. 101 mins.

With: Lewis Stone (Judge Hardy), Mickey Rooney (Andy Hardy), Judy Garland (Betsy), Fay Holden (Mrs Hardy), Ann Rutherford (Polly Benedict), Sara Haden (Aunt Milly)

BABES ON BROADWAY
US 1941

Producer/Arthur Freed. Director/ Busby Berkeley. Script/Fred Finklehoffe, Elaine Ryan. Music/E Y Harburg, Burton Lane, Ralph Freed, Roger Edens, Harold Rome. Photography/Lester White. B&W. GB distribution/CIC (MGM). Certificate U. 118 mins.

With: Mickey Rooney (Tommy Williams), Judy Garland (Penny

Morris), Fay Bainter (Miss Jones), Virginia Weidler (Barbara Jo), Ray McDonald (Ray Lambert), Richard Quine (Morton Hammond), Donald Meek (Mr Stone), Alexander Woollcott (Himself)

WE MUST HAVE MUSIC
US 1942

Off-cut from *Ziegfeld Girl* utilising one Judy Garland number not included in the original film

FOR ME AND MY GAL
US 1942

Producer/Arthur Freed. Director/Busby Berkeley. Script/Richard Sherman, Fred Finklehoffe, Sid Silvers. Music/George W Meyer, Edgar Leslie, E Ray Goetz. Photography/William Daniels. B&W. GB distribution/CIC (MGM). Certificate U. 104 mins.

With: Judy Garland (Jo Hayden), George Murphy (Jimmy K Metcalfe), Gene Kelly (Harry Palmer), Marta Eggerth (Eve Minard), Ben Lue (Sid Simms), Horace McNally (Bert Waring), Richard Quine (Danny Hayden), Lucille Norman (Lilly), Keenan Wynn (Eddie Melton)

PRESENTING LILY MARS
US 1943

Producer/Joe Pasternak. Director/Norman Taurog. Script/Richard Connell, Glays Lehman. Music/Walter Jurmann, Paul Francis Webster, E Y Harburg, Burton Lane, Roger Edens. Photography/Joseph Ruttenburg. B&W. GB distribution/CIC (MGM). Certificate U. 104 mins.

With: Judy Garland (Lily Mars), Van Heflin (John Thornway), Fay Bainter (Mrs Thornway), Richard Carlson (Owen Vail), Spring Byington (Mrs Mars), Marta Eggerth (Isobel Rekay), Connie Gilchrist (Frankie), Leonard Kinskey (Leo), Patricia Barker (Poppy), Janet Chapman (Violet), Annabelle Logan (Rosie), Douglas Croft (Davey)

GIRL CRAZY
US 1943

Producer/Arthur Freed. Director/Norman Taurog. Script/Fred Finklehoffe. Music and lyrics/George and Ira Gershwin. Photography/William Daniels, Robert Planck. B&W. GB distribution/CIC (MGM). Certificate U. 99 mins.

With: Mickey Rooney (Danny Churchill), Judy Garland (Ginger Grey), Gil Stratton (Bud Livermore), Robert E Strickland (Henry Lathrop), Rags Ragland (Rags), June Allyson (Speciality), Nancy Walker (Polly Williams), Guy Kibbee (Dean Phineas Armour), Frances Rafferty (Marjorie Tait), Henry O'Neill (Mr Churchill Snr), Howard Freeman (Governor Tait),

THOUSANDS CHEER
US 1943

Producer/Joe Pasternak. Director/George Sidney. Script/Paul Jarrico, Richard Collins. Musical director/Herbert Strothart. Photography/George Folsey. B&W. GB distribution/CIC (MGM). Certificate U. 126 mins.

With: Kathryn Grayson (Kathryn Jones), Gene Kelly (Eddy Marsh), Mary Astor (Hyllary Jones), John Boles (Colonel William Jones), Ben Blue (Chuck Polansky), Frances Rafferty (Marie Corbino), Mary Elliott (Helen), Frank Jenks (Sergeant Kozlack). Guest appearances by Judy Garland, Mickey Rooney, Red Skelton, Eleanor Powell, Lucille Ball.

MEET ME IN ST LOUIS
US 1944

Producer/Arthur Freed. Director/Vincente Minnelli. Script/Irving Becher, Fred Finklehoffe. Music/Ralph Blane, Hugh Martin. Photography/George Folsey. Colour. GB distribution/CIC (MGM). Certificate U. 113 mins.

With: Judy Garland (Esther Smith), Margaret O'Brien (Tootie Smith), Mary Astor (Mrs Anna Smith), Lucille Bremer (Rose Smith), Tom Drake, (John Truett), Marjorie Main (Katie), Leon Ames (Mr Alonzo Smith), Harry Davenport (Grandpa), June Lockhart (Lucille Ballard), Harry H Daniels Jnr (Lon Smith Jnr), Joan Carroll (Agnes Smith), Hugh Marlowe (Colonel Darly)

THE CLOCK
(GB: UNDER THE CLOCK)
US 1945

Producer/Arthur Freed. Director/Vincente Minnelli. Script/Robert Nathan, Joseph Schrank. Music/George Bassman. Photography/George Folsey. B&W. GB distribution/CIC (MGM). Certificate A. 90 mins.

With: Judy Garland (Alice Maybery), Robert Walker (Corporal Joe Allen), James Gleason (Al Henry), Keenan Wynn (The Drunk), Marshall Thompson (Bill), Lucille Gleason (Mrs A Henry), Ruth Brady (Helen)

THE HARVEY GIRLS
US 1946

Producer/Arthur Freed. Director/

George Sidney. Script/Edmund Beloin, Nathaniel Curtis. Music/Johnny Mercer, Harry Warren. Photography/ George Folsey. Colour. GB distribution/ CIC (MGM). Certificate A. 101 mins.

With: Judy Garland (Susan Bradley), John Hodiak (Ned Trent), Ray Bolger (Chris Maule), Angela Lansbury (Em), Preston Foster (Judge Sam Purvis), Virginia O'Brien (Alma), Kenny Baker (Jerry O'Halloran), Marjorie Main (Honora Cassidy), Chill Wills (H H Hartsey), Selena Royle (Miss Bliss), Cyd Charisse (Deborah)

ZIEGFELD FOLLIES OF 1946
US 1946

Producer/Arthur Freed. Director/ Vincente Minnelli. Music/Roger Edens. Photography/George Folsey, Charles Rosher. Colour. GB distribution/CIC (MGM). Certificate U. 100 mins.

With: Fred Astaire, Lucille Ball, Lucille Bremer, Fanny Brice, Judy Garland, Kathryn Grayson, Lena Horne, Gene Kelly, James Melton, Victor Moore, Red Skelton, Esther Williams, William Powell, Edward Arnold, Marion Bell, Bunin's Puppets, Cyd Charisse, Hume Cronyn, William Frawley, Robert Lewis, Virginia O'Brien, Keenan Wynn

---

TILL THE CLOUDS ROLLS BY
US 1947

Producer/Arthur Freed. Director/ Richard Whorf. Script/Myles Connolly, Jean Halloway. Music/Lennie Hayton. Photography/Harry Stradling, George Folsey. Colour. GB distribution/CIC (MGM). Certificate U. 135 mins.

With: Robert Walker (Jerome Kern), Judy Garland (Marilyn Miller), Lucille Bremer (Sally), Van Heflin (James I Hessler), Harry Hayden (Charles Frohman), Paul Langton (Oscar Hammerstein), Paul Macey (Victor Herbert). Also with: June Allyson, Kathryn Grayson, Lena Horne, Tony Martin, Frank Sinatra, Gower Champion, Cyd Charisse, Angela Lansbury, Ray McDonald

---

THE PIRATE
US 1948

Producer/Arthur Freed. Director/ Vincente Minnelli. Script/Albert Hackett, Frances Goodrich. Music/Cole Porter. Photography/Harry Stradling. Colour. GB distribution/CIC (MGM). Certificate U. 102 mins.

With: Judy Garland (Manuela), Gene Kelly (Serafin), Walter Slezak (Don Pedro Vargas), Gladys Cooper (Aunt Inez), Reginald Owen (The Advocate), George Zucco (The Viceroy), The Nicholas Brothers (Speciality Dance), Lester Allen (Uncle Capuch), Lola Deem (Isabella), Ellen Ross (Mercedes), Mary Jo Ells (Lizarda), Jean Dean (Casilda), Marion Murray (Eloise)

EASTER PARADE
US 1948

Producer/Arthur Freed. Director/ Norman Taurog. Script/Fred Frinkelhoffe. Music/Lennie Hayton. Photography/Charles Rosher, Harry Stradling. Colour. GB distribution/CIC (MGM). Certificate U. 103 mins.

With: Judy Garland (Hannah Brown), Fred Astaire (Don Herves), Peter Lawford (Jonathan Harrow III), Ann Miller (Nadine Hale), Jules Mushin (Francois), Clinton Sundburg (Mike), Jeni LeGon (Essie)

WORDS AND MUSIC
US 1948

Producer/Arthur Freed. Director/ Norman Taurog. Script/Fred Finklehoffe. Music/Lennie Hayton. Photography/Charles Rosher, Harry Stradling. Colour. GB distribution/CIC (MGM). Certificate U. 121 mins.

With: Mickey Rooney (Lorenz Hart), Tom Drake (Richard Rodgers), Marshall Thompson (Herbert Field), Janet Leigh (Dorothy Feiner), Perry Como (Eddie Lorrison Anders), Ann Sothern (Joyce Harmon), Berry Garrett (Peggy Lorgan McNeil), Jeanette Nolan (Mrs Hart). Also with: June Allyson, Judy Garland, Lena Horne, Gene Helly, Cyd Charisse, Mel Torme, Vera-Ellen.

IN THE GOOD OLD SUMMERTIME
US 1949

Producer/Joe Pasternak. Director/ Robert Z Leonard. Script/Samson Raphaelson. Music/George Stoll. Photography/Harry Stradling. Colour. GB distribution/CIC (MGM). Certificate U. 103 mins.

With: Judy Garland (Veronica Fisher), Van Johnson (Andrew Delby Larkin), S Z "Cuddles" Sakall (Otto Oberkugen), Spring Byington (Nellie Burke), Buster Keaton (Hickey), Clinton Sundburg (Rudy Hansen), Marcia Van Dyke (Louise Parkson), Lillian Bronson (Aunt Addie), Liza Minnelli (Baby)

SUMMER STOCK
(GB: IF YOU FEEL LIKE SINGING)
US 1950

Producer/Joe Pasternak. Director/

Charles Walters. Script/George Wells, Sy Gomberg. Music/Johnny Green. Photography/Robert Planck. Colour. GB distribution/CIC (MGM). Certificate U. 109 mins.

With: Judy Garland (Jane Falbury), Gene Kelly (Joe D Ross), Eddie Bracken (Orville Wingait), Gloria De Haven (Abigail Falbury), Marjorie Main (Esme), Phil Silvers (Herb Blake), Ray Collins (Jasper G Wingait), Nita Bieber (Sarah Higgins), Carlton Carpenter (Artie), Hans Conreid (Harrison I Keath)

A STAR IS BORN
US 1954

Producer/Sidney Luft. Director/George Cukor. Script/Moss Hart. Music and lyrics/Harold Arlen, Ira Gershwin, Leonard Gershe. Photography/Sam Leavitt. Colour. GB distribution/Columbia-Warner (Warner). Certificate A. 182 mins (GB; 152 mins).

With: Judy Garland (Esther Blodgett), James Mason (Norman Maine), Jack Carson (Libby), Charles Bickford (Oliver Niles), Tom Noonan (Danny McGuire), Lucy Marlowe (Starlet), Amanda Blake (Susan), Irving Blake (Graves), Hazel Shermet (Libby's Secretary)

PEPE
US 1960

Producer-director/George Sidney. Script/Dorothy Kingley, Claude Binyon. Music/Andre Previn, Dory Langdon, Hans Wittatatt, Augustin Lara. Photography/Joe MacDonald. Colour. GB distribution/Columbia-Warner (Columbia). Certificate U. 195 mins (GB: 170 mins).

Judy Garland sang "The Faraway Part of Town" (by Andre Previn and Dory Langdon while Dan Dailey and Shirley Jones danced. The song was nominated for an Oscar

JUDGMENT AT NUREMBERG
US 1961

Producer-director/Stanley Kramer. Script/Abby Mann. Music/Ernest Gold. Photography/Ernest Laszlo. B&W. GB distribution/United Artists. Certificate A. 190 mins (GB: 178 mins).

With: Spencer Tracy (Judge Dan Haywood), Burt Lancaster (Ernst Janning), Richard Widmark (Colonel Tad Lawson), Marlene Dietrich (Madame Bertholt), Maximilian Schell (Hans Rolfe), Judy Garland (Irene Hoffman), Montgomery Clift (Rudolf Peterson), William Shatner (Captain Byers), Edward Binns (Senator Burkette), Kenneth McKenna (Judge Kenneth Norris), Werner Klemperer (Emil Hahn), Alan Baxter (General Merrin), Torben Meyer (Werner Lammpe), Roy Teal (Judge Curtiss Ives)

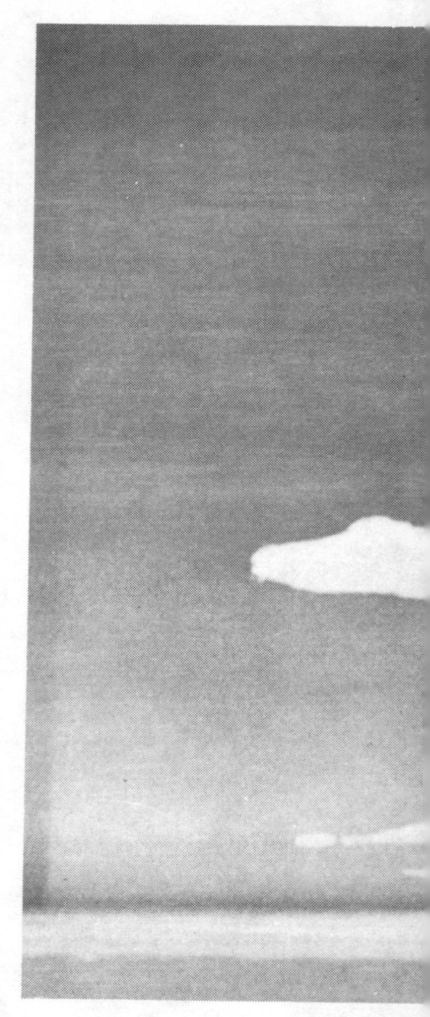

GAY PURR-EE
US 1962

Producer/Henry G Saperstein. Director/Abe Leviton. Script/Dorothy Jones, Chuck Jones. Music/Harold Arlen, E Y Harburg. Photography/Roy Hutchcroft, Dan Miller, Jack Stevens, Duane Keegan. Colour. GB distribution/Columbia-Warner (Warner). Certificate U. 86 mins.

Deft: the "Get Happy" sequence from If You Feel Like Singing

With the voices of: Judy Garland (Mewsette), Robert Goulet (Juan-Tom), Red Buttons (Robespierre), Hermoine Gingold (Madame Ruben-Chatte)

A CHILD IS WAITING
US 1962

Producer/Stanley Kramer. Director/ John Cassavetes. Script/Abby Mann. Music/Ernest Gold. Photography/ Joseph LaShelle. B&W. GB distribution/ United Artists. Certificate X. 104 mins.

With: Burt Reynolds (Dr Mathew Clark), Judy Garland (Jean Nansen), Gena Rowlands (Sophie Widdicombe), Steven Hill (Ted Widdicombe), Bruce Ritchey (Reuben Widdicombe), Gloria McGehee (Mattle), Paul Stewart (Goodman), Elizabeth Wilson (Miss Fogarty), Barbara Pepper (Miss Brown)

I COULD GO ON SINGING
GB 1962

Producers/Stuart Millar, Lawrence Turman. Director/Ronald Neame. Script/Mayo Simon. Music/Harold Arlen, E Y Harburg. Photography/ Arthur Abbetson. Colour. GB distribution/United Artists. Certificate U. 100 mins.

With: Judy Garland (Jenny Bowman), Dirk Bogarde (David Donne), Jack Klugman (George Kogan), Gregory Phillips (Matt), Aline MacMohan (Ida).

Books

There are innumerable press and magazine articles concerning Judy Garland – often described as "autobiographical". Most press reporting (or interviews) is best ignored. However, so much research and detailed writing has emerged in recent years that any reader of this modest offering may use it as a jumping off point, moving on to the following articles and the books listed below. Chapters, extracts etc. may be found in *The MGM Stock Co* by James Robert Parish and Ronald Bowers; *Films in Review* career profile by Robert Rosterman, April 1962; Career portrait by Douglas McVay, *Films and Filming*, October 1961; *On Cukor* by Gavin Lambert; *Easy the Hard Way* by Joe Pasternak; *The Hollywood Musical Film* by John Russell Taylor; *I Remember it Well* by Vincente Minnelli; *Judy Garland* by Noel Simsolo in No 51 the *Antholie du Cinema* series; *Judy Garland and Mickey Rooney: Screen Greats No. 9* published in the USA by Barven – full of attractive photographs. And many more, listed – like so much other invaluable research and information – in *Rainbow Review* (issue 29), which is the official magazine devoted to Judy Garland, published by the Judy Garland Club. Other, more substantial, offerings include:

RAINBOW by Christopher Finch (Michael Joseph). This seems to me the definitive Garland book, lavishly and finely illustrated and produced.

JUDY by Gerold Frank (W H Allen). Another recent, very comprehensive and clear-eyed account of Judy's life and career.

JUDY: THE FILMS AND CAREER OF JUDY GARLAND by Joe Morella and Edward Z Epstein (Leslie Frewin). Attractive and useful for its filmography and contemporary reviews.

THE OTHER SIDE OF THE RAINBOW by Mel Torme (W H Allen). Valuation as a detailed insight into working with Judy – as singer/composer Torme did on the star's twenty-six one-hour television shows.

LITTLE GIRL LOST: THE LIFE AND HARD TIMES OF JUDY GARLAND by Al Di Orio. (Arlington House). A rather over-effusive biography, which also contains a mass of other research, including a detailed discography.

JUDY WITH LOVE by Lorna Smith (Robert Hale). A personal biography which lives up to its title. Not from the pen of a professional writer but from the person who probably knew Judy as well (or better) than anyone else.

JUDY GARLAND, A MORTGAGED LIFE by Anne Edwards (Simon and Schuster). A rather journalistic work, but one that reveals Judy's immense stamina and helps answer the question – how did she survive?

Records

There are so many "new" pressings, reissues and duplications of Garland material that one can only advise the relative newcomer to take care, look out and listen. Only the devoted fan will want some obscure concert or early radio performance, or a collection of songs cut from movies or shows – probably as part of a general LP. Since "advising" on an earlier selected group of discs I do not think there is any change in my thinking – the following dozen records may profitably form the basis of any Judy collection.

ALONE: with the Gordon Jenkins' Orchestra: Capitol. (My personal favourite and – on first hand information – also Judy's).

JUDY AT CARNEGIE HALL – with orchestra conducted by Mort Lindsay. The definitive live show – probably her greatest selling record, on two discs. Capitol.

JUDY: With the Nelson Riddle Orchestra. Capitol. Classic middle period, standards.

A STAR IS BORN: Soundtrack of the definitive version of this show-business movie. Columbia.

JUDY IN LOVE: With the Nelson Riddle Orchestra. Capitol. Middle period, standards.

JUDY GARLAND: THE HOLLYWOOD YEARS. Various orchestras. MGM. Records. Two discs, Indispensable.

MISS SHOW BUSINESS: With the Jack Cathcart Orchestra. A classic record which proves its title.

JUDY GARLAND AND LIZA MINNELLI. "LIVE" AT THE LONDON PALLADIUM. With Orchestra conducted by Harry Robinson. Capitol. Two discs. Great singer, with talented daughter.

THE WIZARD OF OZ. The original cast, soundtrack album. MGM. A must, on grounds of nostalgia and simply because . . .

First published in Great Britain in
1974 by
BCW PUBLISHING LIMITED

Second edition May 1977

ACKNOWLEDGMENTS

The writer would like to thank several people – not least the publishers – for their help on this project. They include John Kobal, Rita Alden, Gillian Hartnoll, the British Film Institute Information Department and, especially, Ken Sephton.

This booklet is – as before – for Søren, who met Judy on his first day in England, 16th September, 1964, and has stayed with us ever since.
Spring 1977

Front cover: At the time of Gay Purr-ee
Frontispiece: A Star is Born

About The General Editor

DAVID CASTELL was born in London in 1943 and educated at Dulwich College. He worked first in advertising, then in magazine journalism. He had contributed film reviews to *The Times Educational Supplement, Illustrated London News,* and *London Life* before, with John Williams, he co-founded the monthly magazine *Films Illustrated* in 1971. After that came BCW Publishing, a company specializing in cinema topics. Mr. Castell reviews regularly for Capital Radio, London's leading commercial station, and was resident host of the BBC television program "Film Night." He contributes writings on cinema to a variety of newspapers and magazines, including the *Sunday Telegraph.* The fourth in a series of annuals he edits, *Cinema '79*, has just been published in the United States.

About The Author

BRIAN BAXTER was for ten years deputy director of the London Film Festival and assistant program planner at London's National Film Theatre where he first met Judy Garland. He has recently joined the BBC in planning of feature films for national transmission.

Baxter, Brian.
The films of Judy Garland / [by]
Brian Baxter. -- St. Paul, Minn. :
Greenhaven Press, c1978.
46 p. : ill., ports. ; 22 cm.
First published in Great Britain in
1974 by BCW Publishing Ltd. ; 2d ed. May
1977.
Filmography : p. 36-44.

1. Garland, Judy. 2. Moving-picture
actors and actresses--United States--
Biography. I. Title